The Legal Framework of the
Modern Company

Titles in the Legal Framework Series

The Legal Framework of the Constitution
Leonard Jason-Lloyd

The Framework of Criminal Law
Leonard Jason-Lloyd

The Framework of the English Legal System
Leonard Jason-Lloyd

The Legal Framework of the European Union
Leonard Jason-Lloyd and Sukhwinder Bajwa

The Legal Framework of the Modern Company
Leonard Jason-Lloyd and Larry Mead

The Legal Framework of Police Powers
Leonard Jason-Lloyd

The Legal Framework of the

Modern Company

Leonard Jason-Lloyd

*Lecturer in Law, University of Derby, and visiting Lecturer in
Law at the Midlands Centre for Criminology and Criminal Justice at
Loughborough University, and the Scarman Centre for the Study of
Public Order at the University of Leicester*

and

Larry Mead

*Senior Lecturer in Law at the University of Derby and
Barrister-at-Law (Lincoln's Inn)*

FRANK CASS
LONDON • PORTLAND, OR.

Published in *1997* in Great Britain by
FRANK CASS & CO. LTD.
Newbury House, 900 Eastern Avenue,
London IG2 7HH, England

and in the United States of America by
FRANK CASS
c/o ISBS
5804 N.E. Hassalo Street
Portland, Oregon 97213-3644

Transferred to Digital Printing 2004

Copyright © Frank Cass & Co. Ltd. 1996

British Library Cataloguing in Publication Data

Jason-Lloyd, Leonard
   The legal framework of the modern company. – (The legal
   framework series)
   1. Corporation law – England
   I. Title II. Mead, Larry
   344.2'0666

                        ISBN 0 7146 4777 2 (cloth)
                        ISBN 0 7146 4288 6 (paper)
                        ISSN 0965-3473

Library of Congress Cataloging-in-Publication Data

Mead, Larry.
   The legal framework of the modern company / Larry Mead
   and Leonard Jason-Lloyd.
        p.   cm.
   Includes index.
   ISBN 0-7146 4777 2 (cloth) ISBN 0-7146-4288-6 (paper)
   1. Corporation law–Great Britain. I. Jason-Lloyd, Leonard.
   1945- II. Title.
   KD2079.M43   1996
   346.41'066–dc20   96-30826
   [344.10666]   CIP

Contents

1 The History and Purpose of the Company   1

2 Documentation, People and Finance   5

3 Incorporation   7

4 Capital   17

5 Company Securities   21

6 The Raising of Capital by Public Companies   25

7 The Directors and the Company Secretary   29

8 Company Accountability   37

9 Company Democracy   43

10 Insider Dealing   49

11 Takeovers, Mergers and Reconstructions   53

12 Liquidations   55

13 Administration Orders and Receiverships   59

   Glossary   61

   Index   63

1

The History and Purpose of the Company

Trade associations referred to as companies can be traced back to the sixteenth century where they existed as merchants' guilds formed for the purpose of gaining monopolies over certain commodities. A century later joint stock companies emerged which shared some of the characteristics of the modern company except they did not include limited liability for their members. This meant that their private assets could be taken by the company's creditors in order to pay its debts. As a result of the historic collapse of the South Sea Company six months after it was formed in 1711, legislation in the form of the Bubble Act 1720 was passed which made it difficult to form companies and other business associations. It was not until 1825 that this Act was repealed and a gradual improvement was effected in enabling businesses to form companies. Since then many Companies Acts have been passed but the most important today (although not the most recent) is the Companies Act 1985 which had three other statutes passed in conjunction with it, namely, the Company Securities (Insider Dealing) Act 1985 (since repealed – see the Criminal Justice Act 1993, Part V), the Business Names Act 1985 and the Companies Consolidation (Consequential Provisions) Act 1985. A year later three further statutes were passed which are of major importance in company law. They are the Insolvency Act 1986 (which repealed the 1985 Act), the Company Directors Disqualification Act 1986 and the Financial Services Act 1986. As a result of two European Union Directives and our own government's desire to effect other changes in the law, the Companies Act 1989 was passed and, finally, Part V of the Criminal Justice Act 1993 was enacted which completely restates the law on insider dealing (see Chapter 10). The diagram shown in Figure 1 illustrates the standing of current legislation within company law.

Although company law is based largely on statute, there has also been a significant development of case law since the middle of the nineteenth century which still plays an important part in formulating modern company-law decisions in the courts and these will be examined later. Those who wish to create business associations today usually form either partnerships or companies. The former is based on contract and is suitable only for relatively small concerns, therefore the law governing this aspect of business association falls outside the scope of this book. The most important type of modern company is the registered company which can be either public or private and limited by shares. Other registered companies include those which are unlimited or limited by guarantee. There are also chartered and statutory companies which are not registered but formed by Royal Charter and Act of Parliament respectively. There are three main segments that comprise a company: the entrepreneurs who provide the management and leadership skills; the employees who carry out the daily tasks; and the shareholders who provide the capital and constitute both the ownership and membership of the enterprise. It is the shareholders who are protected by limited liability which is the greatest single advantage in forming a company.

Company law therefore endeavours to regulate the many facets of human activity while engaged in the numerous functions associated with this particular type of business association.

FIGURE 1

THE DEVELOPMENT OF COMPANY LAW LEGISLATION

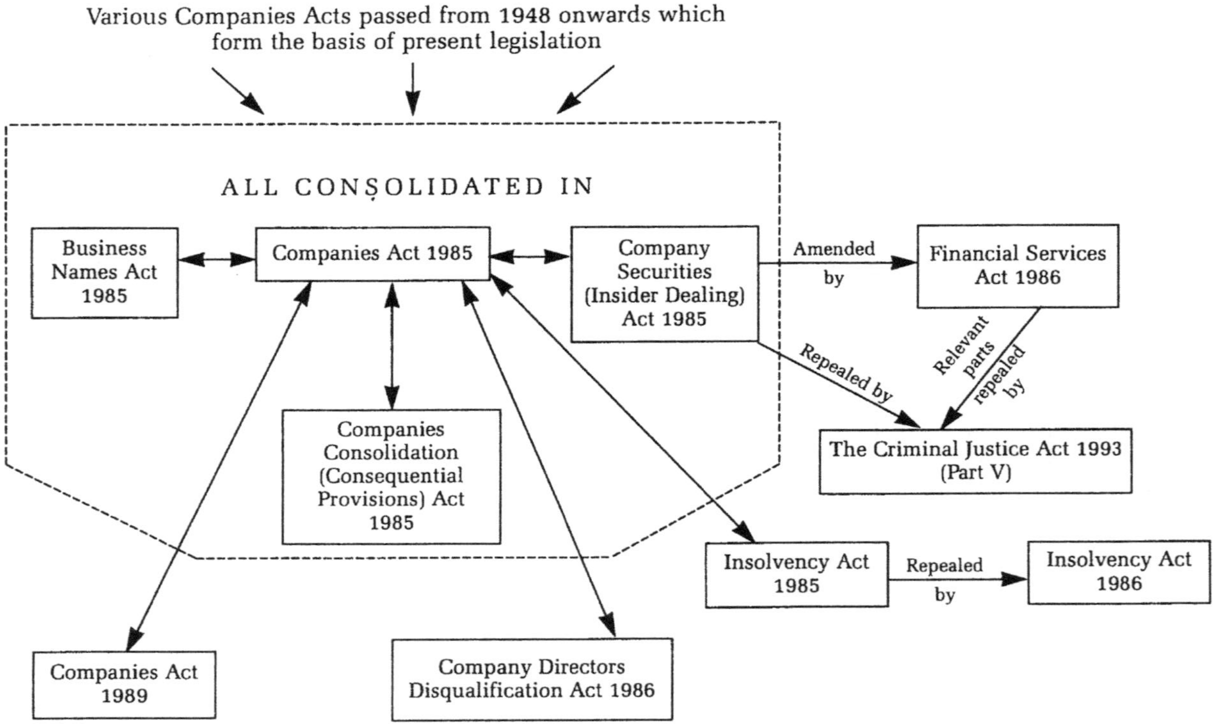

Various Companies Acts passed from 1948 onwards which
form the basis of present legislation

ALL CONSOLIDATED IN

Business Names Act 1985

Companies Act 1985

Company Securities (Insider Dealing) Act 1985

Companies Consolidation (Consequential Provisions) Act 1985

Financial Services Act 1986

Amended by

Repealed by

The Criminal Justice Act 1993 (Part V)

Relevant parts repealed by

Insolvency Act 1985

Repealed by

Insolvency Act 1986

Company Directors Disqualification Act 1986

Companies Act 1989

2

Documentation, People and Finance

A registered company has no physical existence. It is, however, recognised at law and described as a legal person. The company so recognised can sue and be sued, contract, employ persons, have its own bank account and, to a certain extent, have criminal liability.

The need for, and significance of, documentation in the context of this legal person and its activities is great. Certain standard documents must be submitted to the Registrar of Companies in order to form the company and obtain a Certificate of Incorporation. These include a Memorandum of Association, the content of which is discussed in the next Chapter. Articles of Association which constitute the company's rules must also be identifiable. The registered company must maintain numerous registers including a register of members, a register of directors and the company secretary, and a register of charges. Such registers are available for inspection. Events at formally held meetings must be recorded in minutes, and financial information can be discovered in the accounts of a company.

The rights, duties, obligations and roles of physical

persons who act within the corporate entity and who, to a notable extent, are responsible for the company's documentation production and content, are important in gaining an initial overview of the company and its functioning. The company can only contract with outsiders through the actions of the company's directors who are its agents. The role of the shareholders or members as controllers of the company is of great significance. The relationship and relative positions of the directors and members is also of importance. When considering the internal workings of the company – the procedural and administrative aspects – the role of the company secretary should be borne in mind.

Finally, the financial aspects in relation to the corporate entity are worth noting before looking more specifically at the legal framework of the company. Money can be raised on the allotment of shares. Borrowing is another means of raising funds, and the creation of debentures and charges are relevant factors where company indebtedness arises.

While documentation, people, and financial issues can be singled out in providing a brief initial foundation of company law, obvious overlaps exist, and it is not suggested that these categories are exhaustive.

3

Incorporation

PROMOTION

Usually the first step in the formation of a company is the process known as 'promotion' where a person engages in persuading others to contribute capital to the proposed company which is intended to fulfil a specific end. The promoter of a company is also one who runs it initially and often such persons are on its first board of directors. If someone assists a promoter in a paid, professional capacity, such as an accountant or solicitor, they are not classed as a promoter. The duties of promoters are not contained in statute but have been developed through case law where, among other factors, it has been established that they owe a fiduciary duty to the company being formed. This means that they are entrusted with its guardianship and must not, for instance, make a secret profit from their duties. Furthermore, they commit a criminal offence if they deliberately make misleading statements while endeavouring to raise capital for the new venture. An interesting feature regarding promoters is the question of their payment for services rendered. Since the company does not legally exist before incorporation, it cannot enter into any contract which includes any agreement regarding the remuneration of the promoter. However, since promoters are generally the first directors of the new company, this problem is usually obviated. Alternatively, the promoter may sell property to the company above its true value and the subsequent profit will constitute his remuneration. This question of pre-incorporation contracts can present problems to the promoters that may not be so easily resolved, however, particularly with regard to entirely new ventures or where the promoter is not selling his business to a company and is also not a director and majority shareholder. In the case of *Kelner v. Baxter (1866)* the promoters of a company which was being formed to buy an hotel signed a contract on behalf of the proposed company for the supply of some wine. Following the formation of the company this wine was consumed but the company went into liquidation before payment was made. The court held that the promoters were personally liable and it made no difference even if the company tried to ratify the contract made prior to incorporation.

THE CONSEQUENCES OF INCORPORATION

The most important feature of the company once it is incorporated is that it becomes a separate legal entity. In effect it becomes a legal person in its own right and is separate from all the segments that comprise its workings including its members. It is this factor that ensures limited liability for the shareholders. The leading case which firmly established this principle was *Salomon v. Salomon (1897)*. Mr Salomon (senior) ran a one-man business and decided to form a limited company. The company (now a separate legal entity) paid him £39,000 which consisted of 20,000 shares of £1 each, £10,000 in debentures and the remainder in cash. A year later the company went into liquidation, but once Mr Salomon's debentures were paid there was nothing left for the unsecured creditors who alleged that they took priority since Mr Salomon and the company were the same. The House of Lords held that Mr Salomon was entitled to priority of payment because he and the company were separate legal entities. Mr Salomon can also be seen as the promoter of the company (see above). This consequence of incorporation where the company becomes a separate legal entity and subsequently its members are immune from liability beyond the full nominal value of their shares, has been compared to a veil or shield. This 'veil of incor-poration', while protecting members from liability for company debts, highlights the distinction between members as the controllers of a company and the company as an entity. The courts have held that two people who were the only shareholders and directors of a company could be convicted of theft from what was in effect their company. Likewise, it has been decided that a person who owned all the shares in a company except one, could not pay cheques made out to the company into his own bank account, nor could the largest shareholder in a company have an insurable interest in property of that company. There are occasions when this veil can be lifted by the courts such as when a company has been engaged in fraudulent or wrongful trading or used to enable a person to evade his or her legal duty. Instances of where the veil can be lifted are found both through the findings of the courts, and in statute.

Every company must have two documents containing its overall regulations. The first, and most important, is called the Memorandum of Association which specifies the company's constitution and objects which are of particular interest to outsiders who propose to have dealings with it. Because the registered company is recognised as a separate legal entity from its members and is a legal person, it can be liable in contract and tort, and can also in some instances be criminally liable. The company can only function with the involvement of physical persons acting as its agents or employees. The second document is known as the Articles of Association which deals with internal management and administrative matters. The Memorandum must contain the following six clauses:

(1) The Company Name

There are precise legal rules under the Companies Act 1985 governing the selection and use of names by companies. The last word of a private company must end with the word 'Limited' or 'Ltd' and public companies must end with 'Public Limited Company' or 'PLC'. There are exceptions to this rule that only apply to private companies limited by guarantee or to those which promote, for instance, art, science, commerce, charity, religion or any professions which by nature are non-profitmaking. Certain names may not be used which are the same, or very similar, to those already registered, and names will not be accepted which are offensive or likely to constitute a criminal offence. Furthermore, there are restrictions on names that may give the impression of connections with central or local government or royalty, and a name including the words 'British' or 'National' may not be used if it gives an unjustifiable image of superiority or the company is not largely British-owned. The Secretary of State for Trade and Industry has certain powers to direct a company to change its name including instances where similar names are used. However, in such cases there are set time-limits for the Secretary of State to act. If an aggrieved party discovers a name similar to its own being used by another company which falls outside the scope of this power there is a civil remedy available to them. This is called a 'passing off' action. Current legal rules also stipulate how and when the name must be displayed such as outside its place of business and on letter headings, invoices and cheques.

(2) The Registered Office

Every company must have an official address which is its registered office and this must appear on business letters and order forms. It does not have to be located at the actual place of business and often the premises of the company's accountants or solicitors are used for this purpose, since it is primarily the address where official communications can be served in addition to a place where company registers and other documents are kept. These include the register of members, directors, secretaries and debenture holders. Accounting records, minute books and (where applicable) directors' service contracts are among other important documents that are kept at the registered office. Certain rights are vested in members, creditors, debenture holders, directors and even the public in certain instances to examine specific categories of registers and documents.

(3) The Objects Clause

Every company must state its objects in the

Memorandum, thus defining the limits of its business activities. Until the passing of the Companies Act 1989, if a transaction went outside the scope of the objects it was regarded as 'ultra vires' (meaning beyond the scope of the company's power) and subsequently rendered void. This meant that outsiders could find that their contracts were unenforceable, and companies themselves felt too constrained under this rule. Since 1989 the 'ultra vires' rule has been completely liberated for outsiders, who now have complete protection. There are, however, partial restrictions within the company whereby members can bring legal proceedings to restrain directors from making decisions outside the objects of the company unless it already has legal obligations to do so arising from its previous actions. However, it is still possible for the company to ratify 'ultra vires' decisions by special resolution or even to state in its objects that it is to carry on business as a general commercial company, thus giving it the widest possible scope. If none of these applies, members may still sue the directors but even then a further special resolution can be passed removing their liability. If that should fail, it is now permissible for a company to indemnify its directors against such liability, thus avoiding personal financial hardship on their part.

(4) Limitation of Liability Clause

The company's memorandum must state whether the liability of its members is either limited or unlimited. There are two forms of limited liability. The first, and by far the most popular, is the company limited by shares where its capital is divided into shares and the members are only liable for the amount paid or unpaid on those securities. The second type of limited company is one which is limited by guarantee where members agree to an amount which they are prepared to pay should the company be liquidated. This sum is usually very small and applies mainly to companies mentioned earlier that are formed for charitable or educational purposes. There are also a few unlimited companies where their members are personally liable for any unpaid debts. The only significant advantage inherent within such organisations is that they enjoy greater privacy since they do not have to deliver copies of their accounts to the Registrar of Companies.

(5) The Capital Clause

This clause states the amount of the company's capital and the way its shares have been divided. For example, it may state 'The share capital of the company is £100,000 divided into 100,000 shares of £1 each'.

(6) The Association Clause

In this clause each subscriber signs the Memorandum and declares his desire to be formed into the company, taking the number of shares shown against his name. The subscribers are the first directors of the company and must consist of a minimum of two.

The Articles of Association deal with the internal rules of the company such as members' voting rights, the conduct of meetings, the appointment and powers of directors, the company secretary's powers and duties, the payment of dividends and the transfer of shares. If the content of the Articles and Memorandum of a company conflict, it is the Memorandum content which will prevail. Companies limited by shares can adopt a model form for their Articles known as Table A which is part of the Companies (Tables A to F) Regulations 1985 and consists of 118 paragraphs. Many companies merely use Table A as a basis for drafting their own Articles, although under the Companies Act 1985 if a company does not register Articles, Table A will automatically apply, so long as the company is limited by shares. An unlimited company and a company limited by guarantee is required under statute to register its own articles. Subject to the provisions of the Companies Act 1985, the Memorandum and Articles, when registered, bind both the company and its members as if they had been signed and sealed by all of the members. These documents can therefore be seen as forming a contract binding on the members.

With exception of the country of incorporation contained within the registered office clause, any part of the Memorandum and Articles may be changed by special resolution or sometimes by written resolution. But in order to prevent alternations being used for dubious purposes, such as an attempt to commit acts that would be oppressive to the minority of shareholders, certain safeguards are contained within the Companies Act 1985. For instance Section 5 provides that a minimum of 15 per cent of shareholders can apply to the court to have an alteration to the Memorandum cancelled. Also, any alteration to Articles must be bona fide and in the best interests of the company as a whole. An alteration must not increase the financial liability of any member or members to the company. Further, any member may pursue an action under section 459 of the Companies Act 1985 on the basis that the company's affairs have been or are being conducted in a way which is unfairly prejudicial to members' interests generally or the interests of some part of its members.

4

Capital

As mentioned in the previous chapter, the company must state the amount of its capital in the Memorandum. This figure, however, constitutes its nominal (or authorised) capital which represents the maximum number of shares it is authorised to issue and their individual value, although in practice a company need not issue all of them. Shares which have been distributed to members constitute allotted (or issued) capital and this is far more important than nominal capital because it is this total sum for which members are liable to contribute to the company whether or not they are fully paid at the time. Shares do not always have to be paid in full at the time of their issue since this can be done in phases or instalments and on rare occasions their total value need not be paid at the outset. The actual amount paid is called paid-up capital and it is this figure that companies must refer to on their stationery if they make reference to their capital. Uncalled capital is the name given to the amount unpaid on issued shares which is rare these days due to its unpopularity among both investors and companies alike. The chart shown in Figure 2 illustrates the relationship between the various types of capital in four different situations. Companies can increase their share capital so long as the company Articles permit it and the appropriate procedure is followed. A reduction of capital is generally prohibited. The Companies Act 1985, section 135, does provide an exception to this prohibition. However, a special resolution and also court approval is required. The court cannot condone an earlier capital reduction.

A company may change the capital clause in its Memorandum by passing an ordinary resolution provided it has authority in its Articles. There are also two main legal rules which protect capital. The first covers provisions designed to prevent the watering down of capital as it enters the company. The second covers provisions designed to prevent capital leaving the company. The watering-down provisions include statutory rules governing such matters as underwriting commission, brokerage and methods of payment for shares. The measures designed to prevent capital leaving the company once received include reducing capital using the authority of company meetings, the issue of shares at a premium, the acquisition by a company of its own shares, financial assistance for the acquisition of its own shares plus market and off-market purchases of its own shares.

The acquisition of a company of its own shares is prohibited. A number of exceptions do nevertheless exist. A company can acquire its own shares by way of gift. An acquisition can be recognised where there is a forfeiture or surrender of shares on a member's failure to meet a call. A company can issue redeemable shares, as a result of which acquisition will occur on the redemption. Further, the purchasing by a company of its own shares is permissible so long as one of the appropriate statutory procedures is pursued. When a company does acquire its own shares, they must be cancelled or transferred within a limited time period. A company cannot be a member of itself.

A private company can use its capital on an acquisition of its shares. Capital can, however, only be used to make up a shortfall between the actual sum required and other money available for the purchase. A procedure laid down in statute must also be followed. This requires the provision of a Declaration of Solvency, an independent report, the passing of a special resolution, and the recognition of a mandatory period during which the company is prevented from acting on the resolution, pending any objection to the capital usage which may be made.

Statute prohibits the provision of financial assistance by companies for an acquisition of their own shares. This general prohibition does not apply to private companies so long as the provision of assistance is preceded by the completion of a procedure laid down in statute. This procedure is similar to that appropriate where the usage of capital by a private company on the acquisition of its own shares is intended. The Companies Act 1985, section 153, contains a number of exceptions to the general prohibiting rule. Under this section dividend payments are permitted, and also the provision of assistance where such provision is not the main purpose of the transaction. The provision of assistance is also permitted if such provision is part of a larger transaction.

FIGURE 2
EXAMPLES OF ISSUED CAPITAL

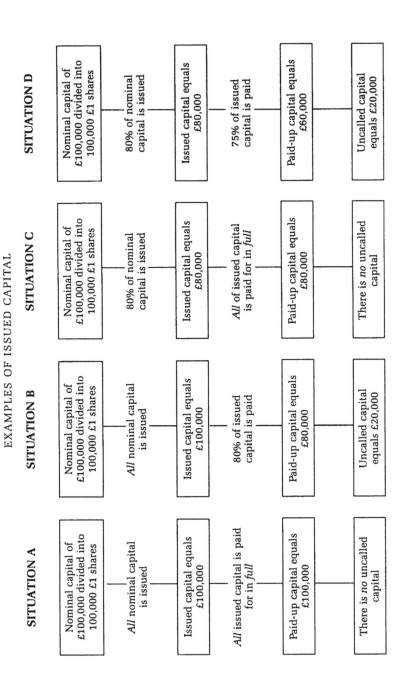

5

Company Securities

Shares and debentures are the two main types of company security. Share ownership means automatic membership of the company, affording voting rights and eligibility to attend meetings. A debenture holder is not a member but a creditor of the company because he or she has made a loan to it a fixed rate of interest whether profits are made or not.

Shareholders run a greater risk than debenture holders who not only receive interest regardless of the company's profitability but also receive priority over shareholders regarding repayment of their investment should the company fall into financial difficulties. However, shareholders can benefit from a major share of the profits if the company prospers. A compromise between the two are preference shares where investors receive a fixed rate of dividend (provided a profit is made) and generally receive priority over other shareholders both in receiving a dividend and repayment of their capital should the company be liquidated. Preference shareholders, unlike debenture holders, are entitled to vote at company meetings although usually on a restricted basis compared to holders of ordinary shares.

The rights of shareholders on matters such as dividends or voting are found either in the Memorandum,

Articles or within the actual terms of the share issue and can only be altered by the agreement of varying proportions of members at company meetings, depending upon the nature of the proposed variation. However, a minimum of 15 per cent of shareholders within the particular class affected can apply to the court to have such a variation cancelled. Among the other rights of shareholders there are also pre-emption rights under the Companies Act 1985. This states that a company must offer ordinary shares to existing shareholders before allotting them elsewhere.

FIXED AND FLOATING CHARGES

It is usual for debenture holders to receive security for their loans and this is in the form of a fixed or floating charge over the company's assets although a combination of both can apply. A fixed charge is a mortgage on such assets as land, buildings, or fixed plant and machinery and these cannot be disposed of without consent. A floating charge applies to future assets since it is not attached to any specific item at the time it is made. If the company defaults then a floating charge will convert to a fixed charge (i.e., it 'crystallises') and debenture holders can then make a claim on whatever asset is most appropriate. Floating charges are advantageous to the company because it can freely deal with its assets without permission from the debenture holders. Also, if it has little or no fixed assets but a substantial stock-in-trade, it can charge property which is unsuitable for a fixed charge. However, the main disadvantage to the lender is that, due to the fluctuation in the value of the assets charged, their value is uncertain.

A company which creates a charge, or acquires property which is subject to a charge, has a duty to deliver to the Registrar of Companies particulars of the charge. Any person interested in the charge can, however, satisfy this obligation. The Registrar is required to maintain a register containing information of such charges. A charge will be void if it is not registered. Likewise, if the information registered is not complete and accurate the charge will be void to the extent that rights are not disclosed. A register of charges must also be kept by every company identifying instruments creating or evidencing charges over the company's property. A copy of such instruments must also be maintained.

6

The Raising of Capital by Public Companies

The Financial Services Act 1986 contains many provisions designed to protect investors who buy securities in public companies. These companies are formed in order to raise capital from the public whereas private companies usually raise funding either from banking organisations or their own membership. Issuing houses (generally merchant banks) play a major role in the process of raising capital from the public. Even if the company makes a direct offer to the public it will still have to be underwritten by an issuing house should the issue prove unsuccessful. In the case of a company making an offer for sale; it transfers all the securities to an issuing house which then sells these to public investors at a slightly higher price. Another method known as 'placing' occurs when an issuing house either places the shares in the capacity as agent of the company receiving commission on each sale (i.e., brokerage) or will subscribe for shares then sell them at a slightly higher price. Under section 89 of the Companies Act 1985 public companies must give their existing shareholders first refusal when issuing new shares, proportionate to their shareholding at the time.

This is known as a 'rights issue'. Securities may not be quoted (or listed) on the Stock Exchange if its Council believes it would be detrimental to investors, or the issuer has not complied with its obligations regarding a listing elsewhere within the European Union. There are strict legal rules regarding listing particulars, especially in respect of advertisements and registration where criminal sanctions can be applied. Recently, many prominent private companies have re-registered as public. This has given rise to the common expression 'going public'. The flow-chart depicted in Figure 3 gives a simplified illustration of the process by which this transformation occurs.

FIGURE 3

HOW A PUBLIC COMPANY CAN DEVELOP

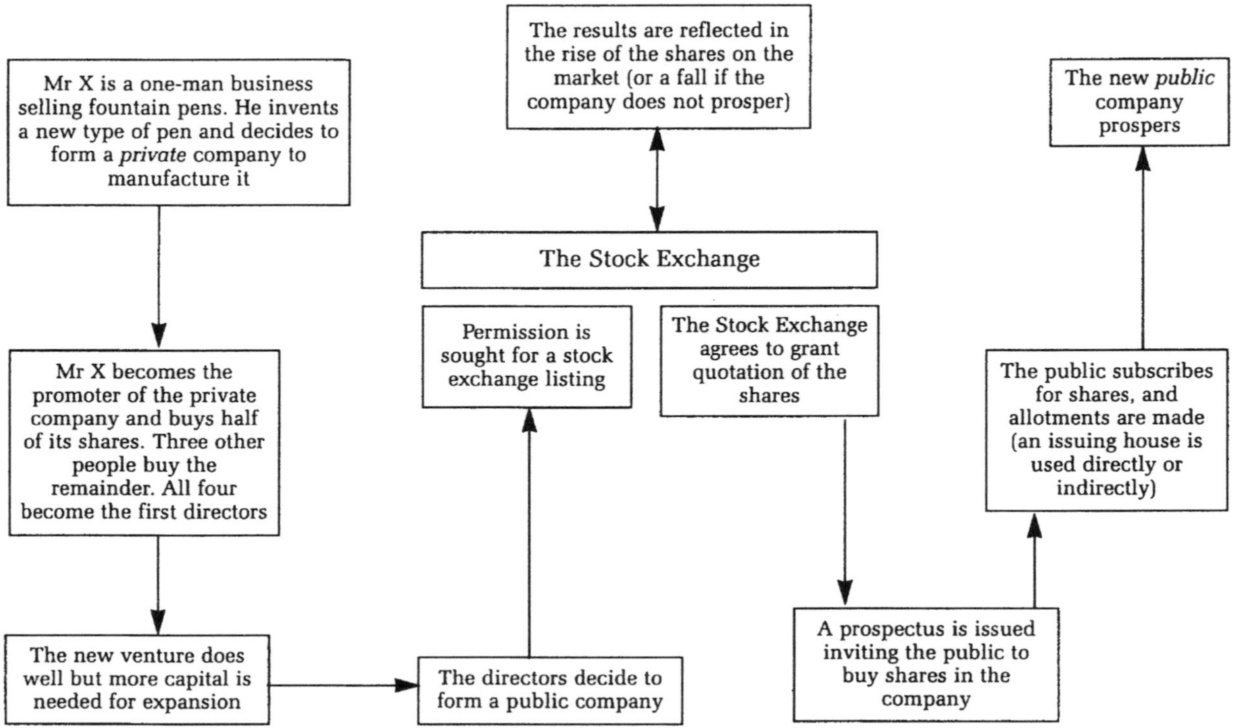

7

The Directors and the Company Secretary

DIRECTORS AND COMPANY MANAGEMENT

There is a general recognition that while a company's shareholders enjoy a position of control, the directors have powers of management. It is important, however, not only to consider the properly appointed director, but also any parties who involve themselves in company management, when considering who in fact at law would be regarded as a director. Surrounding circumstances can also play a significant part in determining those who make up the company's directorate. While a director is a manager, a party acting as manager can similarly be deemed a director. A recognition of the actions of individuals rather than their strictly formal status as directors is shown in legislation such as The Environment Protection Act 1990 which contains a provision that, where a company commits an offence under the Act with the consent of, or because of the neglect of, a director or other senior officer, then he or she, as well as the company, may be punished. No distinction is made between these parties identified as directors, senior officers and managers who have the same responsibility and duty.

THE STATUTORY DEFINITION

In the Companies Act 1985, section 741, some assistance is given in determining the meaning of the word 'director'. Section 741 (1) states: 'in this act, "director" includes any person occupying the position of director, by whatever name called'.

The same definition appears in section 251 of the Insolvency Act 1986 and section 22 (4) of the Company Directors Disqualification Act 1986 for the purposes of those statutes. Any individual should be regarded as a director where authorisation to act on behalf of the company has been given, and management participation is permitted. Even without such authorisation, involvement in company management could satisfy the section 741 definition.

DIRECTORS AND MANAGEMENT

Under regulation 70 of the model form Articles of Association found in Table A of the Companies regulations (Table A–F) 1985, directors are given general powers of management. The extent of director powers generally and the specific powers of directors can be affected by the Articles of Association being altered. Under section 9 of the Companies Act 1985 a special resolution is required on a valid alteration to the document.

It can be vitally important to consider where

shareholder power lies. Is it with one or a few people in a private company or is the membership extensive? Also, where a shareholder or group of shareholders with significant voting power endeavour to participate in company management and override the wishes of formally appointed directors, such control over actions which generally fall to the directors may justifiably give rise to a claim that the shareholder/shareholders are shadow directors.

The directors as managers can regulate their proceedings as they wish subject to the company's articles. In relation to delegation of management powers, regulation 7 of the model form Articles provides that directors may delegate any of their powers to any committee consisting of one or more directors. They may also delegate to any managing director, or any director holding any other executive office, such of their powers as they consider desirable to be exercised by that director. Any such delegation may be made subject to any conditions the directors may impose, either collaterally with or to the exclusion of their powers, and may be revoked or altered. Further, the directors may, by power of attorney or otherwise, appoint any person to be agent of the company for such purposes and on such conditions as they determine, including authority for the agent to delegate all or any of their powers.

DIRECTORS' POWERS AND DUTIES

The directors constitute the directing will of the company and in conjunction with the secretary and the senior managers they are regarded as its officers. Subject to certain conditions a private company may only have one director whereas a public company must never have less than two. Directors owe a fiduciary duty to the company which means that they are held to be virtual guardians of this legal entity, occupying a special position of trust and confidence. Persons appointed subsequent to the incorporation of a company are usually accepted as directors by ordinary resolution at a general meeting. Sometimes vacancies occur between meetings, therefore casual posts can be filled which may be ratified at the next general meeting. Not all directors have to buy shares in their company unless the Articles demand it. Shares held by directors under these terms are called 'qualification shares'.

DISQUALIFICATION OF DIRECTORS

Certain persons are not allowed to be appointed as directors of a company. These preclusions are covered by the Company Directors Disqualification Act 1986 which can disqualify someone from holding office if he or she has been convicted of an indictable offence (namely a crime serious enough to be heard before a jury) in connection with the promotion, formation, management, liquidation or receivership of a company. This also applies if they have been guilty of fraud or breach of duty to the company or have frequently failed in their duty to file important documents with the Registrar of Companies. Directors may also be disqualified as a result of the insolvent liquidation of a company where it is discovered that they have proved unfit to manage a company by virtue of conduct which has caused the insolvency. This does not apply to directors who have genuinely tried to avoid insolvency but have failed. In extreme cases a director may be disqualified for a maximum of 15 years. There are also rules precluding undischarged bankrupts from holding office as directors. If such a person acts in that capacity he commits a criminal offence unless permission has been given by the court.

Directors have the authority to legally bind the company without incurring personal liability and such acts are still valid even if there is a technical defect in their qualification or appointment. The removal of directors be effected by ordinary resolution despite any contrary provision in the Articles or any agreement between the director and the company. They are given the opportunity to make written representations to the members before the meeting and may speak on the resolution at the meeting. Directors automatically vacate office if they are absent from board meetings for more than six months without permission or they become of unsound mind. Unless they have a service contract with the company, directors are not regarded as its servants, therefore their remuneration is usually approved by the company during a general meeting although the board may fix the remuneration of its managing director. The general powers of directors are that they may manage the company and act on its behalf. If the members disagree with the actions of the directors they cannot usurp their function, but they can either alter the Articles to modify their future conduct or remove them by ordinary resolution. However, as mentioned in Chapter 3, directors who act outside the scope of their powers may have their acts approved by special resolution. A special resolution may also relieve directors of any subsequent personal liability for such actions, although if the members do not approve the directors can be liable to make good any loss to the company. This is an essential safeguard to prevent recent legislation which liberated the old 'ultra vires' rule being used to commit fraud.

A director commits a criminal offence if he or she buys or sells options in the listed securities of his or her own company or group of companies. This is an aspect of insider dealing because such activity will be motivated by knowledge not widely known to other investors which could affect the future price of those securities (see Chapter 10). There are also strict legal rules regarding private loans to directors by the company. It is the general rule that neither a public nor private company may make a loan to any of its directors or those within the same group. Furthermore, public companies, or groups which include a public company, may not make (with a few exceptions) indirect loans to its directors or anyone closely connected with them such as their spouses or children. Again, with a few exceptions, the same rules apply to credit transactions and directors who break any of these rules commit a criminal offence. Special provisions exist where a loan is made to a director if his company is a bank or other money-lending organisation. These include the general restrictions that the amount does not exceed £100,000 and the terms must be the same as for another person of similar standing who did not have such a relationship with the company.

Mention was made earlier that directors owe a fiduciary duty to the company. This is a special position of trust and good faith since they constitute its guardians. It should be remembered that a company is only an artificial legal entity which needs the directing will of human beings and the principal actors in this role are its directors. Such a task is not easy since they have to achieve a balance between all the competing interests that a company embraces. For instance, they are expected to consider the interests of both its employees and members which can often be in conflict. Furthermore, directors must avoid a conflict which affects their own interests and must therefore account to the company for any profits made in the course of their duties.

Therefore, in order to satisfy the fiduciary duties which attach to them, directors must exercise their powers for the purpose for which they were given, and avoid their own personal interests conflicting with the interests of the company. Fiduciary duties are owed to the members as a body and the members, if they wish, can waive a breach of such a duty. A director who is also a shareholder can vote to waive his own breach of duty. Further, in circumstances where a director in breach of a fiduciary duty is a majority shareholder, he can actually waive his own breach of duty. A waiver will not be valid where it amounts to a fraud on the minority shareholders. In addition to the fiduciary duties owed, directors owe a duty of care. In considering whether or not a director is in breach of this duty, account is taken of the individual's knowledge and experience. A director can seek relief from the court, in which case it is necessary to establish both honesty and reasonableness in his conduct.

THE COMPANY SECRETARY

Every company must have a secretary who is usually appointed by the directors who determine his terms and also have the power to remove the office-holder. It is usual for public companies especially to comply with the minimum standards laid down in the

Companies Act 1985 regarding company secretaries. These include membership of one of several recognised professional bodies, such as the Chartered Association of Certified Accountants and the Institute of Chartered Secretaries and Administrators or they may be qualified lawyers. Alternatively, suitable persons with the necessary experience as an assistant or deputy secretary may be eligible. A company secretary is often a director as well (although a sole director may not also hold the position of secretary). The position of secretary constitutes the chief administrative function within a company but not the management of it. He may not, for instance, borrow money on the company's behalf nor enter into contracts except on matters that fall under his administrative duties, such as employing staff or purchasing office furniture and equipment. However, the secretary owes the company the same fiduciary duty as its directors.

The status of the company secretary has changed somewhat over the last hundred years, although the ability of the company secretary to contract on behalf of the company remains very limited. His role in relation to the organisation of company meetings, maintenance of company registers, and obligations in relation to share documents and minutes of meetings serve to put in perspective his position within the company. Under the Companies Act 1985, section 744, the secretary is an officer of the company, and in some instances therefore enjoys the same position as a director.

8

Company Accountability

There are many ways in which a company must be accountable to the world at large, particularly those who wish to invest in or deal with it. There are, however, provisions relating to the publicising of certain aspects of its affairs in order to give protection to those who are contemplating, or already have, a business relationship with the company.

COMPANY RECORDS

The first requirement is that the company must maintain certain registers for inspection and they are usually kept at its registered office. These documents include the registers of directors and the secretary, also the members, debenture holders and the directors' interests, if any, in the company's securities. The minute book of general meetings, any directors' service contracts and the company's accounts are among other essential records maintained for possible inspection at the registered office. Certain information must also be lodged with the Registrar of Companies. These include the Company's Memorandum and Articles, the address of its registered office, particulars of the directors and secretary, a statement of its capital, and annual accounts and the annual return which will both be mentioned later. Any ordinary resolutions passed which affect important matters such as the appointment or removal of directors, a change in the registered office, removal of auditors, increases in nominal capital or changes in the composition of shares, also have to be notified to the Registrar. In turn the Registrar must publish the substance of certain documents either received or issued by him in the London Gazette which is a publication scrutinised by various elements in the business world.

Companies are required by law to file an annual return with the Registrar which must be signed either by the secretary or a director. This document constitutes a broad overview of the company and includes such matters as the company's name and registered office address, its principal activity, particulars of the directors and secretary, the amount of issued capital, a list of past and present members and (if a private company) a statement, if applicable, that it has either dispensed with the holding of annual general meetings or dispensed with the laying of accounts and submission of reports at AGM.

COMPANY ACCOUNTS

All companies must maintain ledgers, cash-books, receipts and all other accounting records necessary to prepare their financial statements which include the balance sheet and profit and loss account. The Companies Act 1989 has imposed more stringent rules regarding the accounts and accounting records of the company in which minimum standards are stipulated regarding their efficiency and disclosure, although the new Act introduces a relaxation in the requirement for private companies to lay accounts at general meetings. As mentioned earlier, by passing an elective resolution private companies may dispense with this procedure although the accounts must still be sent to the members and the Registrar. In addition to the financial statements of the company, other documents must be included such as the directors' and auditors' reports.

Small and medium-sized companies now have different rules regarding the submission of accounts since the Companies Act 1989 requires that they need only file modified financial statements with the Registrar. Small companies are defined as private companies which satisfy at least two of the following criteria: a maximum of 50 employees, a maximum turnover of £2m or a balance-sheet total of no more than £975,000. Medium-sized companies are private companies which fall under at least two of the following: a maximum of 250 employees, a turnover not exceeding £8m or a balance-sheet total not in excess of £3.9m.

The new Act further requires that if a company has subsidiaries, group accounts disclosing the state of affairs and profit and loss of both the company and its subsidiaries must be laid before the company at the general meeting although there are a number of exceptions to this rule.

These new provisions regarding group accounts are the result of two European Union Directives. Another important document relevant to company accountability is the directors' report which must accompany the annual accounts when laid before a general meeting. This contains an overview of the general progress of the company, the proposed dividend, the names of the directors and future plans regarding the business of the company.

AUDIT

The process of audit is an essential safeguard against fraud or other malpractice. All companies (except those which are dormant) must have auditors who are appointed by the members at each general meeting where accounts are laid, and they hold office until the next meeting. If a private company decides to dispense with the requirement to appoint auditors annually by elective resolution, the retention of its auditors will remain until they either wish to leave or the company replaces them. Auditors must be fully qualified before they are allowed to act in that capacity. Membership of recognised professional bodies such as the Institute of Chartered Accountants or the Chartered Association of Certified Accountants is now required. Such organisations are regarded as recognised qualifying bodies which also act as recognised supervisory bodies and are thus responsible for providing both the appropriate qualifications for auditors and the essential supervisory role in maintaining minimum professional standards. It is essential that auditors are impartial in carrying out their duties and precise rules exist that are designed to obviate any conflict of interests, such as a close connection between an auditor and persons who may control the company, or an auditor having a financial interest in the company.

An auditor may be removed by the company at any time by ordinary resolution but is entitled to make representations in person at the next meeting where either his normal term would have expired or where a casual vacancy caused by his removal is to be filled. Auditors may also resign at any time provided their written notice contains a statement that their resignation is not connected with any matter which should be a cause for concern of the members or creditors of the company and if such circumstances do exist they should be stated. Either way a copy must be sent to the Registrar and, if it is adverse, to every member and debenture holder of the company concerned. A statement of circumstances now also applies to every instance where an auditor ceases to hold office even if removed.

It is not the place of auditors to comment on the efficiency or profitability of their client company since their main duty is to assess and report its true financial position. Any officer of the company who deliberately makes a false statement to an auditor which is intended to deceive, commits a criminal offence. While the legal obligations of the company to its auditors are precisely stated, so too are the rules relating to the duty of care and skill owed by the auditors to their client company. One of the most important requirements is that auditors should look beyond the figures contained in the accounting records and examine them with an enquiring mind and, where necessary, question apparent discrepancies. Failure to do this can result in legal action being taken against them as in the case of *Thomas Gerrard & Sons Ltd (1968)* where the company's managing director falsified the accounts by altering invoices and including fictitious stock. As a direct consequence this caused the company's profits falsely to appear more favourable than they really were and a dividend was declared which would not have been done had the true financial position of the company been stated. This also resulted in additional tax being paid by the company. The court held that the

41

auditors were liable to repay the dividends plus the cost of recovering the extra tax and also the non-recoverable tax because they failed to follow-up their initial suspicions.

9

Company Democracy

COMPANY MEETINGS

An important means of ensuring democracy within a company is the many provisions contained within the Companies Acts regulating meetings of shareholders. All companies (except private companies that have opted for an elective resolution) must hold an annual general meeting. These are so fundamentally important that if a company fails to hold one the Secretary of State may order it to be held on the application of just one member. The main elements of an AGM usually include the declaration of a dividend, examination of the accounts together with the auditors' and directors' reports, the election of directors where necessary and the appointment of the auditors. Extraordinary general meetings may be called by the directors as they think fit although a certain percentage of shareholders can demand that they call one. Apart from AGMs and EGMs a third category of meeting exists, namely, class meetings. These are attended by holders of a specific class of shares only and are usually convened to consider a variation in their rights.

The legal rules covering company meetings are thorough but complicated. Generally, there must be minimum periods of notice before meetings and some notifications must, when necessary, fully describe the resolutions to be moved. The conduct of meetings is also subject to precise legal rules. For instance, a minimum number must be present and the proceedings properly controlled by a chairperson who is obliged to follow a code of conduct designed to enable all points of view to be expressed and for the business of the meeting to proceed in an orderly manner. Voting is usually conducted by a simple show of hands and works on the principle of one vote for each member. The number of shares they each hold is irrelevant unless a poll is requested, in which case the member usually has one vote for each ordinary share. Every member is allowed to nominate a proxy to attend a meting and vote on their behalf. A person appointed as a proxy need not be a member of the company.

There are three types of resolution to be found in company meetings: ordinary, special and extraordinary. Ordinary resolutions apply where either the Articles or other rules do not stipulate that a certain matter be dealt with by special or extraordinary resolution. The removal of auditors or directors as mentioned earlier are examples of .matters that come under ordinary resolution. Special resolutions cover such decisions as a change of the company's name, alterations of the Articles, reduction of capital or the approval of an ultra vires act.

Extraordinary resolutions also cover very important company decisions but differ from special resolutions since a shorter period of notice is given. Instances where extraordinary resolutions must be used are when the company proposes to be voluntarily liquidated due to the inability to pay its debts, and to authorise the liquidator to make compromise arrangements with the creditors. The Companies Act 1989 has further simplified procedures in meetings for private companies in two instances. The first has been partially covered in Chapter 8, under the rules regarding elective resolutions in respect of dispensing with the laying of accounts before the company in a general meeting. Elective resolutions go beyond that in so far as other formalities may be waived such as the requirement to appoint auditors annually and even the holding of annual general meetings in their entirety. Elective resolutions must be passed at a meeting of the company but can be revoked by ordinary resolution.

Another reform of private company meetings introduced by the 1989 Act is the provision for written resolutions which can be passed by members without the necessity of holding a meeting. Certain matters may not be dealt with in this way, such as the removal of directors or auditors because in these instances they would be deprived of the right to make oral representations at the meeting.

The extent to which resolutions are introduced in formal meetings can vary because of a number of factors. In this regard the public company and private company can be validly distinguished. The size of membership can also be significant. At one extreme a company may have thousands of members, whereas a private company, now, need only have one member.

MINORITY SHAREHOLDER PROTECTION

Another means of ensuring democracy within a company is through the concept of minority protection in which both statute and case law ensure that the majority of members do not rule oppressively against the minority. Although much power is vested in the directors, the ultimate control of the company lies with the majority of shareholders, if they can be mobilised in a single purpose such as controlling the composition of the board and altering the Articles. An important case which illustrates the need for safeguards to protect the minority is *Foss v. Harbottle (1843)* where some directors sold their land to the company at an exorbitant price and two of its members brought an action to compel them to make good the loss to the company. The court held that action should be taken against the directors using a majority decision at a general meeting. Exceptions to the *Foss v. Harbottle* rule, which effectively supports the idea of majority rule, do exist. Where a minority pursue an action where fraud or illegality are identified, the claim can succeed. Likewise the failure by a company to obtain the requisite support needed to be able to act in a particular way, can form the basis of a successful minority action. Beyond this, a minority action can succeed where justice demands that it should. In order for a common-law action to succeed, and the *Foss v. Harbottle* rule to be validly opposed, the minority must satisfy the maxim that 'he who comes to equity must come with clean hands'. In other words, no element of wrong in relation to the claim must attach to those pursuing the claim.

Minority protection is also found in the Companies Act 1985 and the Insolvency Act 1986 which include the following provisions: the right of at least ten per cent of shareholders to require the Department of Trade and Industry to investigate the affairs or ownership of a company; the right for members to requisition an EGM; the right of members to demand a poll; the right for a member to petition the court to liquidate a company on just and equitable grounds; and the right for a member to apply to the court where the company's affairs are being unfairly conducted in a prejudicial manner. Furthermore at least 15 per cent of the shareholders can object to an alteration of the objects of the company and there is also case law which prevents a fraud on the minority. Any one member can petition the court for a winding up of the company on the grounds that it is just and equitable to do so. The court then has the power to agree to a winding up order or not. No other remedies are available. A claim of unfairly prejudicial conduct can also be brought by any one member, and in this instance the court has a wide discretion when introducing a remedy.

10

Insider Dealing

Insider dealing is a criminal offence punishable by a maximum of seven years' imprisonment and an unlimited fine when tried on indictment. Those who commit this offence are not only acting in a manner which is unfair to investors generally but their activities can be very damaging to the reputation of the securities market. Insider dealing was previously covered by the Company Securities (Insider Dealing) Act 1985 with amendments contained within the Financial Services Act 1986. The law regarding this offence has now been restated within sections 52 to 64 of the Criminal Justice Act 1993 in conjunction with schedules 1 and 2. Under this statute, an individual will be guilty of insider dealing if he deals in price-affected securities that are linked to information he possesses as an insider, or if he encourages another to deal in the same securities. The 1993 Act defines a number of key elements within the above definition. For instance, 'inside information' is described as information that is specific and precise and therefore not of a general nature which, if made public, would be likely to affect significantly the price of any securities. The new Act further states that information of this nature is to be regarded as 'price-sensitive' and that the relevant securities are to be classed as 'price-affected'. An 'insider' is defined as a person who is aware that he has inside information from an inside source as a result of being a director, employee, or shareholder or an issuer of securities. This also extends to persons who have access to this information by virtue of their employment, office or profession. The 1993 Act further states that a person will be regarded as a direct or indirect source of inside information once he knows that it falls within this category.

An example of insider dealing can be illustrated in the case of *R v. Jenkins (1987)* where the private secretary to a company chairman obtained information that the company was going to make a take-over bid for another firm. The private secretary then made an attempt to deal in the shares of that firm just prior to the announcement of the bid.

Since it is not the intention of the current legislation to impede the normal processes of the stockmarket, there are a number of exceptions to the legal rules regarding insider dealing. These now come under the heading of either defences or *special* defences. The former includes the reasonable belief that the information had been sufficiently widely disclosed, or that the defendant would have acted in the same way even if he or she did not possess the information. Examples of special defences include instances where an individual acts in good faith in his business as a market maker (or someone employed in such a business).

Under the Criminal Justice Act 1993 prosecutions for alleged insider dealing offences must be initiated or approved by the Director of Public Prosecutions or the Secretary of State.

(The reader is recommended to read the article

'Insider Dealing – The New Law' written by Leonard Jason-Lloyd in the December 1993 edition of the *Business Law Review*. This article explains in detail the new legal rules governing insider dealing.)

11

Takeovers, Mergers and Reconstructions

TAKEOVER BIDS

Takeovers occur when a bidding company acquires enough shares in another company to gain control over it. The company intended to be taken over is known as the 'target company'. Such an action is sometimes resisted by the directors of the target company and occasionally there can be more than one bidding company. Takeovers can be beneficial to the target company, especially if it is under-performing and could be improved by a change of management, although in certain instances investors have not benefited from a takeover when the new board and controlling members have sought to use it to further their own interests. There are a number of legal rules governing takeovers designed to protect the minority of dissenting shareholders in the target company and also to ensure that its directors do not abuse their fiduciary duty and either make a secret profit or issue new shares in order to try to obstruct the bid. Furthermore, there is the City Code on Takeovers and Mergers which contains rules governing the general conduct of companies during takeovers. One example is that shareholders in the target company must be informed by its directors as soon as it is known that a bid is going to be made for it. A merger (or amalgamation) differs from a takeover because it usually occurs only when the directors of both companies are in agreement. Mergers occur when two companies join together either under the name of one of them or alternatively use the name of a new company which has been specifically formed for this purpose.

RECONSTRUCTIONS

A reconstruction constitutes the means by which a company reorganises itself without involving an existing company. For example, its directors may form a new company and then transfer to it all the assets of the previous business venture with little or no change in the management of the new company.

12

Liquidations

Liquidation means the phasing-out of a company and the process through which its assets are disposed of in order to pay its members and creditors. Another term for liquidation is 'winding-up'. Although not all liquidations occur because of insolvency (such as when a new company is formed as part of a reconstruction and the previous company is wound-up), most liquidations become necessary due to companies being unable to pay their debts. There are two main categories of liquidation: voluntary and compulsory.

VOLUNTARY LIQUIDATION

Voluntary liquidations are the most prolific and exist either as creditors' voluntary liquidations or members' voluntary liquidations. In the latter instance members must first pass the appropriate resolution at a general meeting and appoint a liquidator who, once in office, takes over the powers of the directors unless he or she, or the members in general meeting, sanction otherwise. However, before the decision to liquidate is initially put to the members, the directors must make a formal declaration that the company will be able to pay its debts within 12 months and this declaration of solvency must then be sent to the Registrar of Companies. If a declaration of solvency is not filed with the Registrar then the liquidation becomes a creditors' winding-up. Generally, the liquidator's powers in both forms of voluntary winding-up are very similar to those vested in him during a compulsory liquidation which come under the general heading of doing whatever is necessary to wind-up the company and distribute its assets. This includes, among other things, selling its property. If at any time during the winding-up the liquidator believes that the declaration of solvency cannot be fulfilled then he must call a creditors' meeting and the process then becomes a creditors' voluntary winding-up. This form of liquidation will occur anyway when a company passes a resolution to wind-up but it is not possible for the directors to make a declaration of solvency, in which case the company must hold a meeting of its creditors within 14 days. The process of a members' voluntary liquidation ends when the liquidator lays the final accounts before a meeting of members and the company is usually then dissolved three months later. The same occurs in a creditors' voluntary winding-up with the addition of a separate meeting for the creditors.

COMPULSORY LIQUIDATION

Compulsory liquidations, which are conducted under the auspices of the court, are relatively slow and expensive. There are a number of grounds for winding-up a company in this way but only two will be examined here as the others rarely occur. The first ground on which a company may be wound-up compulsorily is where it is just and equitable to do so. This includes instances where there are serious problems at board level and in consequence the directors have lost confidence in each other or are so antagonistic towards each other that they are unable to make important company decisions or are managing the company in such a manner as to justify a lack of confidence in them. However, like all equitable decisions in the courts, the judges decide such cases on their own merits in the light of what is reasonably considered to be fair and just. The most common ground for a compulsory liquidation is simply because a company cannot pay its debts. A company will fall into this category if it fails to meet a debt of more than £750 within three weeks after receiving a demand for payment, or fails to satisfy a court order for this amount, or the court is satisfied that it generally does not have the means to pay its creditors. Creditors are the most common petitioners in such cases although the court can disregard them if the majority in value of the other unsecured creditors oppose this move.

Initially, the official Receiver assumes the role of liquidator but following a series of prescribed steps he is eventually replaced by an insolvency practitioner who takes on the full responsibility of the liquidator. Once the court order has been made the directors' powers cease. All legal actions against the company for debt are stopped (although other actions may continue), but the company may be allowed to continue its business in whole or part if a better price can be obtained for its assets as a result. Furthermore, some of the company's employees may be allowed to continue working for it if their presence is of benefit to the liquidator. An important feature of all forms of liquidation is the priority of debts. The first to be settled are the costs of the liquidation; second are the

preferential debts which include PAYE, VAT and
National Insurance contributions which have fallen
due and arrears of employees' salaries (up to £800);
third are the creditors secured by floating charges;
fourth are the unsecured creditors; and fifth, any
amount due to the members.

13

Administration Orders and Receiverships

Administration orders are a relatively new process by which companies in financial difficulties may possibly be rescued in whole or part or alternatively have their assets disposed of more profitably than would be the case if liquidation or other forms of insolvency proceedings were used. An application to petition the court for an administration order can be made by the directors, members or one or more creditors. The court must be satisfied that the company is unable to pay its debts and that the order is likely to achieve its intended purpose. Once the application has been made the company may not be liquidated nor may legal proceedings be taken against or by the company without permission of the court and once the order takes effect the Administrator manages the entire affairs of the company. Within three months of the administration order, the Administrator must send a statement to the creditors and members (plus the Registrar of Companies), containing the proposals for achieving its aims. This statement must later be presented to a meeting of creditors during which they may suggest any changes.

However, if they cannot agree then the court may discharge the administration order or make any other order it thinks fit. Similar action can also be taken if any member or creditor makes an application to the court on the grounds that the Administrator is managing the company to their detriment in an unfairly prejudicial manner. If the creditors agree with the Administrator's proposals at the outset of the meeting, they may appoint a committee of creditors who will act as a liaison body between the creditors as a whole and the Administrator. If, during the administration process, the business recovers, then its management is returned to the directors; failing that liquidation is the usual course of action.

If a company fails to pay interest on debentures or defaults on another term of the trust deed then it is usual to appoint a Receiver to sell the assets subject to the charge and repay the debenture holders. A Receiver is a term which generally describes a person who carries out a receivership where property has been used as security for a loan under a fixed charge, whereas the relatively recent term Administrative Receiver refers to someone who is acting as a Receiver under a floating charge.

Whenever a Receiver is appointed the company is usually forced into liquidation but it is possible for both a Receiver and liquidator to function concurrently when the company is being wound-up if debenture holders wish to enforce their rights. In such cases the Receiver must take second place since the liquidator is required to represent the best interests of the creditors and contributories as well as the debenture holders.

Glossary

Fiduciary Duty – A special duty of trust and good faith owed by directors and company secretaries to a company.

Registrar of Companies – A senior official within the Department of Trade and Industry responsible for the issuing of official documents to companies, maintaining or deleting their records and enabling examination of certain company documents by the public on request.

Ultra Vires – A decision taken outside the scope of a company's powers.

Declaration of Solvency – A declaration by directors that in their opinion the company will be able to pay its debts as they fall due for the ensuing 12 months.

Index

Accountability 37
Accounts 38
Administration Orders 59
Administrators 60
Administrative Receivers 60
Amalgamation 54
Annual General Meeting 43
Articles of Association 5,10, 13, 37
Association clause 13
Audit 40–42

Bubble Act 1720 1
Business Names Act 1985 2

Capital 17–19
Capital clause 13
Capital, raising 25
Certificate of Incorporation 5, 7
City Code on Takeovers and
  Mergers 53
Companies Act 1985 1, 10, 14, 18,
  22, 30
Companies Act 1989 2, 12, 38, 44
Companies Acts – diagram 4
Companies Consolidation
  (Consequential Provisions) Act
  1985 2
Companies (Tables A–F)
  Regulations 1985 14
Company Accounts 38
Company Acquisition of Own
  Shares 18
Company Director's
  Disqualification Act 1986 2, 32

Company Limited by Guarantee 14
Company Records 11, 37
Company Secretary 35
Compulsory Liquidation 56
Conflict of Interest 35
Creditors 56
Creditors' Meeting 56
Criminal Justice Act 1993 2, 49

Debentures 21
Democracy 31, 43, 46
Department of Trade and Industry 46
Directors 6, 30
Director Disqualification 32
Dividends 21

Elective Resolution 43, 45
Extraordinary General Meeting 43,
  46
Extraordinary Resolution 44

Fiduciary Duties 35
Financial Assistance 19
Financial Services Act 1986 2, 25,
  39
Fixed Charges 22, 60
Floating Charges 22, 60
Flotation, company (diagram) 27
Forfeiture 18

Going Public 25, 26
Guarantee, limited by 10

History 1

Incorporation 7–8
Insider Dealing 49
Insolvency Act 1986 2
Insolvency Practitioner 57
Issued Capital 17
Issuing House 25

Legal Entity 8
Limitation of Liability 12
Limited Company 10
Liquidation 55
Liquidator 56–57
Loans to Directors 34
London Gazette 38

Meetings 43
Memorandum of Association 10,
   14, 37
Mergers 54
Minority Shareholders 45
Modified Financial Statement 39
Mortgages 22

Name, company 10
Nominal Capital 17
Notice, meetings 44

Objects Clause 12
Officer 36
Official Receiver 57
Ordinary Resolutions 18, 44

Paid-up Capital 17
Placing 25
Preferential Debts 58
Price-sensitive Information 49
Private Company 19
Promotion, company 7
Public Limited Company (PLC) 10

Qualification Shares 32

Raising Capital 25
Receivership 59–60
Reconstructions 54
Records 38
Reduction of Capital 18
Registers 5, 7, 37
Registered Office 11
Registrar of Companies 5, 23, 37
Registered Company 2,
Resolutions, meetings 43
Rights Issue 26

Secretary, company 35
Secretary of State, Trade and
   Industry 11
Securities 21
Shareholders 21, 25
Shareholders, minority 45
Shares 21, 25
Small Companies 39
Special Resolutions 44
Surrender 18

Takeovers 53
Target Company, takeovers 53
Trade Associations 1

Ultra Vires 12
Uncalled Capital 17
Unfairly Prejudicial Conduct 15, 47
Unlimited Company 14

Voluntary Liquidation 55
Voting, meetings 44

Written Resolutions 45

For Product Safety Concerns and Information please contact our EU
representative GPSR@taylorandfrancis.com
Taylor & Francis Verlag GmbH, Kaufingerstraße 24, 80331 München, Germany